BLACK
COMMUNICATION

Robert W. Mullen
Northern Kentucky University

UNIVERSITY
PRESS OF
AMERICA

LANHAM • NEW YORK • LONDON

Library of Congress Cataloging in Publication Data

Mullen, Robert W.
    Black communication.

    Bibliography: p.
    1. Afro-Americans–Communication. 2. United States
– Race relations. 3. Persuasion (Rhetoric) I. Title.
P94.5.B552U565 1982   001.54'08996073   82–42547
ISBN 0–8191–2543–1
ISBN 0–8191–2544–X (pbk.)

To

Dianna

One Day at a Time

Live and Let Live

Easy Does It

ACKNOWLEDGMENTS

Originally titled The Rhetorical Strategies of Black Americans in 1980, materials in this revised edition are based upon chapters in An Analysis of the Issues Developed by Select Black Americans on the War in Vietnam, Ph.D. dissertation, 1971, The Ohio State University, by Dr. Robert W. Mullen, and originally copyrighted in 1971 by University Microfilms, Ann Arbor, Michigan.

CONTENTS

Oppression evolves a logic of its own. An
ideology, though weird, often means more than
it says.

> Gordon W. Allport,
> Foreword to The Black
> Muslims in America, 1969

INTRODUCTION

The Study of Black Rhetoric

Black Americans, in seeking to establish
a meaningful role and identity in American society,
wrote and spoke with persuasive force on human
rights in every era beginning with the colonial
period and extending to the present. Black
rhetoric has been with us for a long time. It
is only now after either choice or pressure that
we have come to realize its rich history.

There is a phenomenon known as a black
rhetoric, messages generaged by blacks and for
blacks in the attempt to gain status and what
may be called the "good life." By good life is
meant that blacks, too, desire the good things
in life, which so many other Americans have
already gained; things now taken for "granted"
by the white middle class.[1] It can also mean
aspiring to a place in an open society--"one in
which integration is a free option rather than
a faint hope."[2] For Martin Luther King the term
good life meant "a share in the American economy,
the housing market, the educational system and
the social opportunities." For King, it meant
to "'get in' rather than to overthrow."[3] For
Bobby Seale, the good life means the same goals
the white man fights for. These are simply a
decent education, good jobs, and good housing.[4]
In terms of economics alone, Stokely Carmichael
explains the term this way: "We want our people
to be able to enjoy life and to get all the things
they need for a decent life without having to
struggle as hard as they now do."[5] Expressed
in social terms, Carmichael says:

> I guess we want what most people want out
> of life: people who are happy and free
> and who can live better than they now live

1

and who make and participate in decisions
that affect their lives, and never feel
ashamed of the color of their skin or
ashamed of their culture.[6]

Politically, the term means for Carmichael a
black people "free of oppression."[7]

In this attempt to obtain the good life,
blacks throughout history have also made meaningful and fitting responses to the exigencies
that confronted them. As Golden and Rieke point
out in their text The Rhetoric of Black Americans,
the total concept of black rhetoric may be viewed
largely as a persuasive campaign with periods
of revolt and terror.[8]

A focus on black rhetoric is justified
for at least three major reasons. First, it
has made an impact on both black and white
America. Secondly, it will not be a momentary
thing. And, third, its strengths and weaknesses
as a movement are of value to the communication
scholar. Still further, its justification, as
Golden and Rieke suggest, rests on the following:

1. It has fashioned leaders and heroes.

2. It has created a body of literature.

3. It has given the young black American
a new sense of self-identity.

4. It has altered attitudes and images.

5. It has questioned the accepted norms
of speech and the traditional doctrines of
usage.[9]

In short, black rhetoric is an identifiable and
useful study in itself. Since black history in
America has been what Arthur L. Smith calls, "a
history of protest" and "a history of communica-
tive challenges," an assessment of the rhetorical
management of those challenges seems important.

Among gains to be realized for the black student is a greater sense of the worth and dignity of his past. For the white reader, a deeper understanding of the black individual and a basis to communicate with him. For society in general, there should be an increased appreciation of why America today is bordering on turmoil.[10]

4

NOTES: INTRODUCTION

[1] "Black America 1970," *Time*, 6 April 1970, p. 13.

[2] "Report from Black America--A *Newsweek* Poll," *Newsweek*, 30 June 1969, p. 17.

[3] Martin Luther King, *Where Do We Go From Here: Chaos or Community?* Bantam Books (New York: Harper & Row, 1968), p. 153.

[4] Cited in Gordon Parks, "Eldridge Cleaver in Algiers, a Visit with Papa Rage," *Life*, 6 February 1970, p. 25.

[5] Interview with *Sucesos* representative in Cuba, cited in James L. Golden and Richard R. Rieke, *The Rhetoric of Black Americans* (Columbus, Ohio: Charles E. Merrill Co., 1971), p. 524.

[6] Ibid., p. 525.

[7] Ibid., p. 524.

[8] Ibid., pp. 10-17.

[9] Ibid., pp. 3-4.

[10] Arthur L. Smith, "Building a Course in Black History: A Rhetorical Perspective," abstract of paper presented at the 55th meeting of Speech Association of America, New York City, 27 December 1969, pp. 19-20.

THREE PERSUASIVE STRATEGIES

American historians, until recently, have never dealt properly with the black American. Writers have "written patronizingly about him," observed Franklin, "or deplored his sufferings, or all but ignored his presence, treating him as an appendage to American history rather than an integral part of it."[1] Yet, at the birth of America, blacks, too, shared the white man's concept of liberty and expressed it in words and deeds. The Declaration of Freedom presented by blacks to the Massachusetts Legislature in 1777 and the memorial to the first man alleged to fall in the revolution at Boston in 1770, Crispus Attucks, are examples of this. But when independence was finally won, black Americans had to start again their own separate struggle for freedom and equality. That continuing struggle not only is the central theme upon which black history is built, but is a crucial aspect of American history as well. Yet, Americans of all hues know too little about this. And today, when that struggle has become what Franklin and Butterfield term, "the critical social issue of our time," there is now the urgent attempt to understand its beginnings.[2] Indeed, as there has been a tradition of protest and dissension in American history by white Americans to change American society, so, too, the black American has also been a part of this tradition.[3] With a principal dimension of black history encompassed by spoken symbolic interaction,[4] Arthur L. Smith indicates that

> Proclamations of dignity, selfhood, equality, freedom, and justice hav always been the black man's most personal confrontation with the speaking platform. The numbers and varieties of the spokesmen suggest the energy expended in the effort of black

liberation. First, slavery was denounced;
and after the emancipation, the black spokesmen turned their attention to the oppressive
conditions brought on by segregation and
discrimination. The black revolutionists
voice concern over the presence in today's
society of the same racist tendencies that
have existed in the nation since 1619.[5]

Using a number of methods to protest and
achieve goals, black resentment at discrimination
and deprivation was channeled in these ways.
First, in Revolutionary days it was fairly common
for slaves to save enough money to purchase their
freedom or to initiate court suits, some winning
compensation for work done as slaves. Others
in the abolitionist movement sent petitions to
Congress against the Fugitive Slave Act and to
legislatures against segregated transportation
and education.[6] Second, retaliatory violence
was not unknown; it occurred both during the
antebellum years and throughout the century since
emancipation. Third, verbal protests, the use
of the negro vote, picketing and boycottes have
all been direct expressions of the race's frus-
trating experience in America.[7] Fourth, alienated
from the mainstream of American life, some
aggressions were sublimated into nationalist
attempts to create all black communities within
America or to a "waiting-out" or emigration to
Africa and Haiti. Emigration led many blacks
to conclude that it was better for both races
to be separated. Fifth, some black resentment
was suppressed into an accommodating acceptance
of the status quo, "looking to Heaven for solace."
or "internalizing" the white man's view of the
black American. Thus their expression of resentment has depended largely on cultural factors
with each historical period producing certain
types of adaptation.[8]

However little black writesr, speakers,
and thinkers may have exerted an influence on
white American thought over the years,
Martin Luther King writes, in his last book, that

8

it was, nevertheless, the black American who alone "illuminated imperfections in the democratic structure that were formerly only dimly perceived," forcing a reexamination of the meaning of American democracy, both economic and political.[9] "By taking to the streets," King points out, "and there giving practical lessons in democracy and its defaults," the black American has "decisively influenced white thought."[10]

Strategies and Movements

Inasmuch as black history in America has been a history of protest, there are a number of ways from which to view this protest.

Scott and Brockriede write that "traditionally rhetoric has been the study of verbal persuasion."[11] However, now realizing that nonverbal actions or cues such as gestures affect how receivers respond to the verbal discourse, both see black rhetoric as the "special interaction of people in a situation."[12] Since, they argue, "A rhetorical perspective is a way of looking at how men use symbolic behavior to influence other men and events," this implies four dimensions from which the critic may view black rhetoric. First, if the critic approaches black rhetoric as a "transaction among people," he may then study the audience, identification, or the elements of ethos and credibility. Second, approaching rhetoric as a "transaction of ideas," the critic may well study the speaker's rhetorical decisions, philosophical position and stance, the ideology represented, policies advocated, data used, or style developed to be consistent with those decisions. Third, the critic may well make judgments on the speaker's perception of the situation, the choice of channels, or what this situation invited or prescribed. In all, the rhetorical perspective is "a complex set of interacting dimensions" or a "transaction" among people or ideas. A fourth approach is to view the rhetorical stance of the speaker, grouped here as militant, moderate, or conservative.[13]

9

In contrast, additional ways to analyze
black revolutionary rhetoric are suggested by
Arthur Smith. Smith discusses as elements of
black revolutionary rhetoric the tactics of keeping
whites off-balance and the "or-else" threat of
violence.[14] The four rhetorical strategies
Smith offers as ways to analyze revolutionary
rhetoric are: (1) vilification, (2) objectivica-
tion, (3) legitimation, (4) mythication.[15]
Vilification is "the agitator's use of language
to degrade an opponent's person, actions, or
ideas." Objectification is "the agitator's use
of language to direct the grievances of a particular group toward another collective body
such as an institution, nation, political party,
or race." Mythication employs "language that
suggests the sanction of suprarational forces,"
thus creating "a spiritual dynamism" for the
movement and demonstrating "the righteousness
of his cause." Legitimation "is the use of language
to answer the oppositon" and a refutative strategy.
Not only an argumentative rebuttal to an opponent,
it is also a "psychological weapon" that seeks
"to explain, vindicate, and justify the activists
involved in his movement."[16]

Among the fundamental issues probed by
Smith in a theme approach are the claims that
all black people face a common enemy, that there
is a conspiracy to violate black manhood, that
America is a hypocritical country, and that unity
among blacks must be achieved for liberation.[17]

Haroland Randolph analyzes black rhetoric
on the basis of how persons with attitudes favoring
segregation, compromise, integration, or evolu-
tion, use distinctly different arguments to support
their positions. He contends a person may be
labeled a separatist if he argues groups
must maintain their cultural integrity.[18] On the
other hand, Randolph believes the integrationist
can be identified by the tendency to argue people
must be judged as individuals and democracy must
be made to work in America to prove its value
to the world.[19]

The editors of Ebony Magazine divide black rhetoric into the integration approach, the separatist approach, and the course of liberation. Integration is defined as a "reciprocal process" in which

> blacks and whites gravitate toward each other, sharing decision-making control over institutions and communities and melding their ethical and esthetic values. "Integration" . . . implies desegreation or the removal of all legal barriers to the massive coming together of people. Such a process also implies social and cultural exchanges between mutually-respecting equals.[20]

The separatist presses for physical and cultural separation from whites because of the relative "powerlessness" of blacks. The separatist argues that before any minority group can be integrated into the mainstream, its members must first develop economic and political power among themselves so that eventually they can bargain from a position of strength rather than beg because of weakness.[21]

While the white man is central to both integration and separation, either in movement toward or away from blacks, the white man's presence is not crucial to the liberation strategy. Since liberationists perceive the white man as nonexistent, integration becomes

> irrelevant to a people who are powerless. For them the equitable distribution of decision-making power is far more important than physical proximity to white people. Indeed, they want black people to take the dominant role in determining the black-white relationship in America. This means complete emancipation of blacks from white oppression by whatever means . . . necessary.[22]

Some liberationists challenge individualism with the contention that blacks are oppressed as a

group rather than as individuals and must therefore see "communalism as crucial to the needs
of emerging people like the blacks of America
and their suffering brothers elsewhere in the
world."23

Golden and Rieke suggest that the rhetoric
of black Americans throughout history seems
representative of three persuasive strategies:
assimilation, separatism, and revolution. These
categories give a more meaningful introduction
to the broad scope and variety of this rhetoric.
More importantly, however, a description of each
strategy and its particular characteristics is
important as every major rhetorical event falls
under these headings and affects the rhetorical
practice of the men who subscribe to them.
Additionally, each strategy influences the arguments used by particular communicators. To
suggest these strategies alone are all inclusive
would certainly be in error. However, conven-
iently grouping black rhetoric under these three
headings will achieve the following:

1. For blacks, "a greater sense of the
worth and dignity of their past."

2. For whites, "a deeper understanding
of 25 million fellow Americans" and "a basis
to communicate with them."

3. For historians and researchers,
insights into a methodology.24

Finally, it is hoped that under these three
persuasive strategies something will be dis-
closed about "the use of words as instruments
of power."25

Assimilation

The important decade of civil rights
progress, from 1955 to 1965, found its victories
"in an appeal to the conscience, the laws and

12

the pragmatism of white America."26   Four men
can claim as much credit as any for those victories. Thurgood Marshall, Whitney Young, Roy
Wilkins, and Martin Luther King all spoke for
the black citizen to the white man demanding
new efforts in the black American's quest for
equality.

Thurgood Marshall, named in 1967 to be
the first black American to sit on the Supreme
Court, appeared before that same Court thirty-
two times during his twenty-three-year term as
counsel of the N.A.A.C.P. From 1938, Marshall
built a series of victories that culminated in
Brown v. Board of Education, decided by the
Supreme Court in 1954. To win that battle,
Marshall persuaded the Court that separate
schools were "inherently unequal."27

While the N.A.A.C.P., under the leadership of Roy Wilkins, pursued legal goals, the
National Urban League, headed till 1971 by the
late Whitney Young, concerned itself with America's
employers and more jobs for blacks in positions
of the white collar category. In this context,
it may be seen that while the N.A.A.C.P. attacked
on the legal front and the Urban League on the
economic, Dr. King, as head of the Southern
Christian Leadership Conference, considered the
moral stance of the nation.28   More than Marshall,
Young, or Wilkins, King spoke to his own people
with words that, at the same time, were also
meant to be overheard by white America. A dis-
cussion of King alone, his background, speeches,
and writings are, therefore, important as it
reveals both the man's philosophy, and, more
importantly, reflects the essential thrust of
the assimilation strategy.

The late Martin Luther Kings, Jr., was
born in Atlanta, Georgia, in 1929. After grad-
uating in 1948 from Morehouse College and in
1951 from Crozer Theological Seminary, he received
his doctorate from Boston University in 1955
and his Doctor of Divinity in 1959. He was pastor

of the Dexter Avenue Baptist Church in Montgomery,
Alabama, president of the Southern Christian
Leadership Conference, and vice-president of
the National Baptist Convention, Incorporated.
Awarded the Nobel Prize in 1964, he was also
the author of such books as Why We Can't Wait,
Strength to Love, Strive Toward Freedom, and
Where Do We Go From Here: Chaos or Community?
He was assassinated in 1968.29 Robert Storey,
a black attorney with a prominent Cleveland,
Ohio law firm,30 describes below how King was
thrust into the national spotlight in 1955.

> When a black seamstress named Rosa Parks
> refused to yield her seat on a Montgomery,
> Alabama bus to a white man on December 1,
> 1955, it occurred to few people . . . that
> her simple act of defiance of local custom
> would touch off one of the greatest and
> broadest reform movements . . . ever known.
> What southern segregationists saw as an
> act of an arrogant black woman . . . was
> probably best and most perceptively described
> by . . . King when he called it "her intrepid
> affirmation that she had had enough. It
> was an individual expression of a timeless
> longing for human dignity and freedom.31

"It was the genius of King," submits Storey,
"that permitted him to grasp the universality
of Rosa Park's defiance and to help transform
that act into the broadly based civil rights
movement of the late fifties and early sixties."
Under King's leadership, continues Storey,
"blacks and whites, young and old worked
together across religious, economic, and state
lines 'to overcome.'" College students particularly were caught up in the notions of
commitment and participation through sit-ins
and voter registration drives. Through working
with King, the young had come to believe that
they could indeed play an immediate role in
making America a better place for all.32

The Message of Nonviolent Resistance

The Civil Rights Movement of the early sixties by King was an affirmation of hope that injustices accumulated over the years could be eradicated by appealing to the rational and moral sense of the nation. As Storey describes it, the King movement acted out the stated American belief that citizens may effectively petition government for the redress of grievances.[33]

Guided by the concept of nonviolent resistance, there were, according to King, four elements of nonviolent protest. The first was "to use the process of the mind and emotion to persuade your opponent that he is wrong."[34] Arthur Smith details this first element this way:

> King's movement had been based on a fundamental belief in the goodness of man. He insisted that America had the moral courage to correct the injustices perpetuated on the black man. Beyond that, he believed that America would redress the grievances if those injustices were amply shown.[35]

Second, the nonviolent protester did not seek to defeat or humiliate his adversary but rather to win his friendship and understanding. Third, this strategy was centered not against persons but rather against "forces of evil." As King said to the people of Montgomery: "The tension is, at bottom, between justice and injustice. . . . We are out to defeat injustice and not white persons who may be unjust."[36] The fourth point of nonviolence, as advocated by King, was a willingness to accept suffering without retaliation. As King himself explained this:

> He must not only refuse to shoot his opponent but must also refuse to hate him. To retaliate in kind would do nothing but intensity the existence of hate . . . , along the way of life, someone must have

sense enough . . . to cut off the chain
of hate. This can be done by projecting
the ethic of love to the center of our
lives.37

Adding to this fourth point, Smith states that
King's message did not contain the threat of
violence or the implication of "or else." The
only times, concedes Smith, that his rhetoric
even hinted of violence was when he pleaded with
America to accept his nonviolent approach because
rejection could only lead to violence. But,
concludes Smith, "he never intimated that he
would be a party to or a preacher of violence."[38]
As King himself said of violence:

Ultimately a genuine leader is not a searcher
for consensus but a molder of consensus.
I said on one occasion, "If every Negro
in the United States turns to violence,
I will choose to be that one long voice
preaching that this is the wrong way."39

King was concerned that blacks should
achieve full status both as citizens and as
human beings. But he was also disturbed about
"the health of our souls." Therefore, as he
said, he "must oppose any attempt to gain our
freedom by the methods of malice, hate, and
violence that have characterized our oppressors."
He, thus, saw hate as "just as injurious to the
hater as it is to the hated" with humanity
"waiting for something other than blind imitation
of the past." For King, a "dark, desperate,
confused and sin-sick world" waited for this
new kind of man and this new kind of power.40

Self-Image

A Second positive response by the assimilationist to the black dilemma was to develop a
sense of "somebodyness" in the black American.
Here the attempt was made to instruct the black
man on the "disastrous sense of his own worth-
lessness" instilled since the days of slavery.

16

To overcome this feeling of being less than human,
the assimilationist preached that a "sense of
somebodyness" meant the refusal to be ashamed
of being black. Self-acceptance and self-
appreciation was one way to cause white America
"to see that integration is not an obstacle,
but an opportunity to participate in the beauty
of diversity."[41] As King said:

> As long as the mind is enslaved the body
> can never be free. Psychological freedom
> . . . self-esteem, is the most powerful
> weapon against the long night of physical
> slavery. No . . . Kennedyan or Johnsonian
> civil rights bill can totally bring this
> kind of freedom. The Negro will only be
> truly free when he reaches down to the inner
> depths of his own being and signs with .
> . . assertive self-hood his own emancipa-
> tion proclamation.[42]

To gain self-esteem, King urged blacks to say
to themselves and the world:

> I am somebody. I am a person . . . a man
> with dignity and honor. I have a rich and
> noble history, however painful and exploited
> that history has been. I am black and
> comely.[43]

Thus, one strategy of the assimilationist was
to respond to both the white and black view that
blacks were basically inferior, or less than
human.

The Message of Brotherhood

Another part of the assimilationist
strategy was to presume the brotherhood of all
men. This strategy, in terms of audience, saw
the black man speaking directly to the white
man, persuading society at large of the equality
of man. It, thus, viewed the American racial
revolution as "a revolution to 'get in' rather

17

than to overthrow." The following lines from
King are in point:

> We want a share in the American economy,
> the housing market, the educational system
> and the social opportunities. This goal
> itself indicates that a social change in
> America must be nonviolent. If one is in
> search of a better job, it does not help
> to burn down the factory. If one needs
> more adequate education, shooting the prin-
> cipal will not help. . . . To destroy any-
> thing, person or property, cannot bring
> us closer to the goal we seek.[44]

Another feature of this substrategy as
exemplified by King was "the Christian doctrine
that it is sinful to hate."[45] Present sufferings
were always contrasted against the background
of future glory and fugure triumph; the general
theme being "the greater the suffering here,
the greater would be the reward in the world
to come."[46] The difference between the
assimilationist and radical, then, as Eric
Hoffer sees it, springs mainly from their attitude
toward the future.[47] As Hoffer details this
in The True Believer:

> A mass movement has to center the hearts
> and minds of its followers on the future.
> . . . The self-sacrifice involved in mutual
> sharing and cooperative action is impossible
> without hope. . . . On the other hand, when
> everything is ahead and yet to come, we
> find it easy to share all we have and to
> forego advantages within our grasp.[48]

The Strategy of Compromise

A fourth feature of assimilation is
compromise with the white community and its
leaders. While some blacks contend that leaders,
such as King, held their position primarily
because they were acceptable to white leaders,

18

the assimilationist regards compromise as one
of the most practical and effective modes of
adjustment in the existing power situation.49
Conducting their affairs as much as possible
on the basis of moral principles, the
assimilationists' power, to a large extent,
depends on their influence with the white
community.50

August Meier concludes that "not since
Booker T. Washington" has a black leader emerged
with as much appeal both black and white as King.
In Meier's view, King functioned in the early
sixties as the mediator of the diverse wings
of the black protest movement.51

Meier also views King as "amenable to
compromises" and often willing to postpone or
avoid a direct confrontation in the streets.
He was "ideologically committed to disobeying
unjust laws and court orders, in the Gandhian
tradition," but generally followed a policy of
not disobeying Federal Court orders. In all,
says Meier, he profoundly awakened the moral
conscience of America through a combination of
militancy with caution and righteousness with
respectability.52

At the heart of King's influence, notes
Meier, were two additional facts. First, better
than others, he articulated the aspirations of
blacks and "the vision of his dream for them
and for America." Second, he communicated black
aspirations to white America more effectively
than anyone else. His religious terminology
and the Christian symbols of love and nonresistance
were partly responsible for his appeal among
whites as both were "reassuring to the mentality
of white America." King's success with whites
was also built upon white America's "growing
feeling of guilt." His rhetoric, then, played
upon white guilt feelings.53

Unique in that King maintained a balance
between moral appeals and a militant display

of power, his most important function, Meier believes, was that of "effectively communicating Negro aspirations to white people, of making nonviolent direct action respectable in the eyes of the white majority."[54]

In review, then, King's rhetoric tried to identify the interests of blacks and whites and to cooperate with white leadership.[55]

Simons, in summarizing King's pattern of persuasion in the civil rights struggle, develops the view that the strategy of assimilation is the "embodiment of reason in verbal interaction," exemplified by the rhetoric of the courtroom and the conference table, and the method rhetoricians "understand and characteristically prescribe."[56]

Golden and Rieke summarize that the assimilationist message

1. Begins with the premise that blacks are ethnologically equal to whites and, therefore, have to be fully integrated into the American culture.

2. Argues black accomplishments and contributions to America are proof of ethnological equality.

3. Argues the brotherhood of man and the inherent equality of the races.[57]

4. Seeks the "good life" by absorption into society and a faith in the "melting pot" ideal.

5. Contends moral persuasion can effect change.

6. Relies on legislative and judicial action to guarantee freedom under the law and the Christian message and religious argument for su tenance.

7. Makes an appeal to both audiences, black and white.[58]

8. Appeals to the whote anglo-saxon respect for law, justice, and fair play.[59]

In short, this strategy means blacks participating in major ways in the American mainstream.[60] It stresses the average black man does not want to destroy anything. Here it assumes the black man is not "basically opposed to the system; he just doesn't like being at its bottom."[61] Put another way, Lawrence P. Neal, former arts and cultural editor of Liberator, summarizes that the integrationists do not believe the basic socioeconomic structure must be destroyed, but rather, that blacks must simply be given a "greater slice of the capitalistic action." Believing in reform not revolution, these communicators have decided the best course lies in seeking some kind of "rapproachement" with the "system."[62]

Separatism

Since we cannot get along with our former slave masters in peace and equality after giving them 400 years of our sweat . . . and receiving in return some of the worst treatment human beings have ever experienced, we believe our contributions to this land and the sufferings forced upon us by white America justifies our demand for complete separation in a state or territory of our own.[63]

Elijah Muhhammad
Messenger of Allah

This quote serves to suggest that in some ways the legal successes of 1955-1965 "spawned" much of the turmoil of the late sixties, the angry militancy, and the many urban outbreaks. "Implicit in the legal victories was a guarantee

of equality that many white Americans were not
prepared to grant."64 In other words, the prejudice woven into the fabric of society could
not be argued out of existence before the
Supreme Court. The "real restraints" upon
freedom and equality "stood revealed" and many
blacks, therefore, "despaired of ever getting
clear of them."65

   With persistent exigencies, situations
evolved that required different strategies.
The separatist, arguing that observable,
recognizable, persisting exigencies could not
be removed, urged withdrawal or removal from
the American mainstream.

   The rhetoric of separation, in terms of
audience, is primarily black men speaking to
other blacks. With the exception of Marcus
Garvey's "An Appeal to the Soul of White America"
in 1923 and Malcolm X's frequent press and radio
and television interviews, it relies little on
an appeal to the white conscience nor white
acceptance of its message. Termed by some
nationalism, this strategy makes the following
linguistic distinctions. First, separation
means withdrawal or retreat away from the white
man, either outside America, or into enclaves
set up within certain southern states. Second,
nationalism can also mean that regardless of
where the white man lives, blacks must draw
together in developing the new black nation.
The emphasis is also on nationhood here,
establishing a black territory to promote and
develop those unique black qualities such as
language, literature, folkways, and values.
The nationalist also wants to own and control
the economics and politics of the new black state
or community. Arguing it is a separatist society
already, he sees a drawing away from white society
into a separate territory as the best hope for
black survival. Through regrouping or falling
back, later confrontation with the white establishment is possible.

The Black Muslims

C. Eric Lincoln's The Black Muslims in America is an important study of the history, ideology, organizational structure, and methods of the Black Muslims. Lincoln sees the movement as essentially "a religion of protest," a movement of social protest that moves upon "a religious vehicle."[66]

Claiming a membership of close to 100,000 persons, their ultimate demand is that blacks be allowed to set up a separate state within the United States, occuping as much as one-fifth of the nation's territory. Black Muslims are neither pacifists or aggressors. They pay strict attention to the letter of law regarding peace and order. They further engage in no sit-ins, test nosegregation statutes, nor participate in any marches. They do, however, believe in keeping the scores even and they have warned all America that "an eye for an eye" is the only effective way to settle racial differences.[67] Against the backgrounds of lynchings, uncertainty of justice in the courts, the tradition of disprivilege and opposition to first-class citizenship, all are contributory to the making of a Muslim and what Lincoln terms the "Muslim mood."

With its beginnings in the early 1930s, Lincoln defines a Black Muslim as:

> a Black american who is a follower of Elijah Muhammad, "Spiritual Leader of the Lost-Found Nation in the West." Black Muslims are distinguished from orthodox Moslems not in their spelling of the word . . . but in their belief that their leader, . . . Muhammad, is the Messenger of Allah himself, who came in person (under the name of Fard) to wake the sleeping Black Nation and rid them of the white man's age-old domination.[68]

In determining the constituency of the
Muslims through observation and informal interviews, Lincoln concludes that, first, the membership is young with eighty percent of a typical
congregation between the ages of seventeen and
thirty-five. As an "activist" movement, the
appeal is directed to youth. Second, the membership is predominantly male and essentially lower-
class. Attracting few intellectuals, a majority
of the membership is composed of factory workers,
laborers, ex-convicts, dope addicts, and gamblers.
Third, the membership is almost wholly American
negro, predominantly ex-Christian, its members
drawn primarily from a Protestant tradition.
Lincoln notes that the fundamental attraction
of the movement is its emphasis on group
solidarity, its pressure that men acknowledge
themselves as black, and that all blacks work
together to accomplish group aims. These aims,
summed up for Lincoln by one Muslim minister,
are:

> To get the white man's foot off my neck,
> his hands out of my pocket and his carcass
> off my back. To . . . look straight into
> his cold blue eyes and call him a liar every
> time he parts his lips.69

Muslims make no secret of the fact that
they count themselves a part of the growing
alliance of non-white peoples, expected
eventually to inundate the white race, thus,
removing the supremacy whites have enjoyed for
so long.70 The appeal goes deeper with the idea
that every Muslim holds himself ready to die
for his brother, and more especially for his
sister.71

The central theme of the Muslim's is "the
glorification of black civilization and the
deprecation of the white man's culture," which,
whenever adopted by blacks, "has reduced him
to impotence and ignominy." The Muslims have
made "black" the ideal, the ultimate value,
proclaiming blacks to be "the primogenitor of

all civilization, the Chosen of Allah, 'the right-
ful ruler of the Planet Earth.'"[72] Rejecting
white culture and revising history to establish
that today's black men are descended from "glorious
ancestors," the Muslims believe the future will
be better and "the inherent superiority of his
race will triumph and he will again rule the
world."[73]

The Doctrines of the Movement

In developing race consciousness and a
hatred of the white race, the Muslims teach
blacks that they have a "manifest destiny" while
the white man is the "personification of the
evil that separates the Black Man from his
freedom, his moral development and his God."
They further reject the word "negro" as a label
by whites to make discrimination more convenient.[74]
Believing that as long as blacks live among
whites they will be subject to economic and
political abuse, separation, they hold, provides
the only realistic opportunity for mutual respect
between the races.[75] Two basic doctrines are,
first, their insistence that blacks must separate
from the "abhorrent" and "doomed" white race,
and secondly, their belief that it is a manifest
destiny of blacks to inherit the earth.[76]

Goals

Muhammad wants every black in America
reunited with his own forming "a United Front
of Black Men." Second, the Muslims demand
absolute separation of the black and white races
in all relationships. Third, they call for an
entirely separate black economy as a fundamental
aspect of total separation. Last, in terms of
political goals, allusions are made to a separate
nation here in America, sometimes in terms of
three to five states.[77]

The Muslims on Integration

While black audiences are frequently urged
to give the Christian religion back to the white
man and see it as "a religion of slavery,"
audiences, in turn, are also urged to see their
surnames as "badges of slavery."[78] Thus, as
one response to the idea of integration, the
symbol "X" takes on this double meaning:

> implying "ex," it signifies that the Muslim
> is no longer what he was; and as "X" it
> signifies an unknown quality or quantity.
> It at once repudiates the white man's name
> and announces the rebirth of Black Man.[79]

Integration is seen as "a stratagem of
the white man to insure his survival in a world
he has managed badly." The following remark
from Muhammad is in point:

> The white man's time is up, and he knows
> it. He has no friends anywhere. He now
> hopes that by integrating with the rising
> Black Man, he can avoid paying for the long
> list of crimes he has perpetrated against
> humanity. So he has undertaken to "sweet-
> heart" with the only people who are stupid
> enough to listen, the dupes he has trained
> to love him.[80]

The Muslims, thus perceive such other organizations as the National Urban League and the
N.A.A.C.P. as essentially controlled by white
men, both dependent upon white philanthropy.
Opposed to any kind of passive resistance or
sit-in technique, the Muslims rejected King's
philosophy because he emphasized the Christian
principle of loving the oppressor rather than
retaliating aginst him. King, representing
to the Muslims "a capitulation to the cunning
Christian strategy of the white man," is, thus,
scorned for having turned many potential "freedom-
fighting" blacks into "contented, docile slaves."
Muhammad tells his followers never to initiate

26

violence but to retaliate if they are attacked.
He further ridicules whites for demanding that
blacks turn the other cheek, when they themselves
will kill even without provocation. Thus,
Muhammad believes the white man's greatest fear
is that blacks will know the truth about him
and unite against him.[81] In short, the Muslims
consider it futile to reform American society.
Planning simply to retire from it and cultivate
the Black Nation, the Muslims believe whites,
lacking black victims, will then presumably turn
on each other and destroy themselves, leaving
blacks to "inherit the earth."[82]

Malcolm X

The man who spoke most clearly to those
who, despite recent court rulings, still despaired
was Malcolm X. Malcolm was "the central figure
in the attack on nonviolence of action and the
spirit."[83] As Robert Storey saw him, his ideas
converted the biracial civil rights movement
into a "struggle for identity" for the black
masses.[84]

Malcolm was Muhammad's chief lieutenant
in the open affairs of the Muslim movement and
his chief emissary to the Islamic nations of
Africa and Asia. As the most articulate spokesman and organizer for the movement, he directed
and coordinated its program, founded new temples,
conducted rallies, and served as Muhammad's chief
spokesman. Importantly, whereas Muhammad spoke
almost exclusively to the black masses, Malcolm
frequently interpreted the movement for white
society through press meetings, numerous radio
and television interviews, and appearances
at various colleges and universities.[85]

Malcolm's concern was with what he termed
"the collective white man." He wrote: "You
cannot find one black man . . . who has not been
personally damaged in some way by the devilish
acts of the collective white man."[86] Jarring

whites by telling blacks to stop begging favors
from whites and rather get up off their knees
and fight their own battles,[87] Malcolm demanded
that blacks "draw back into themselves,"
especially emotionally, to relearn their African
roots, to merge their efforts for maximum effect,
to assert their manhood as something that they
already have, not as a civil right they must
bargain for.[88] Malcolm could speak to the ghetto
black for he knew the ghetto better than most
black leaders. Malcolm Little had gone the route
from a Harlem hoodlum, thief, dope pusher,
convict, "an avaricious student who devoured
hundreds of books in the prison library," to
a "religious and racial zealot of the Black
Muslims."[89] Adopting the Black Muslim faith
in 1952, he fought for black rights, perceiving
the white man as a "devil." His intellect,
"belying a ninth-grade education, soon made him
the most effective of the Muslim spokesmen."[90]
Questioning much of the simplistic rhetoric of
the sect and particularly the notion that all
whites were by definition the devil, he later
withdrew from the Muslims in 1964. After two
trips to Africa and the Middle East during 1964,
he returned still preaching black power and black
pride, but now more "a man of compassion" seeking
"to ignite the spark of brotherhood in human
beings."[91] He was assassinated in New York City
on February 21, 1965, before he could fully
develop his new stance.

Although the preceding analysis suggests
that Malcolm moved from one strategy to another
with each given exigency, the issue and the goal
for Malcolm remained the "good life." Lifting
the black struggle above the realm of civil
rights alone, Malcolm forcefully argued for

> Human rights! Respect as human beings!
> That's what America's black masses want.
> That's the true problem. . . . They want
> not to be walled up in slums . . . like
> animals. They want to live in an open,

free society where they can walk with their
heads up, like men and women.92

On April 8, 1964, Malcolm gave a speech on "The
Black Revolution" in New York in which he further
detailed what was meant by the black quest for
the "good life." More importantly, however,
he also indicated in what ways the assimilationist
and separatist strategies were alike. He said
then:

> All of our people have the same goals. .
> . . That objective is freedom, justice,
> equality . . . recognition and respect as
> human beings. We don't want to be integra-
> tionists . . . separationists. We want
> to be human beings. Integration . . .
> separation is only a method that is used
> by other groups to obtain . . . equality
> or human dignity.93

For Malcolm, the important thing was not integration or separation, but recognition as human
beings. In fact, he remarked, the actual fight
was not over civil rights but human rights.94
Thus, for Malcolm, the objective of complete
freedom, justice, the "good life," the immediate
recognition as human beings never changed. As
he stated on December 20, 1964, at the Audubon
ballroom in New York City: "I don't care what
you belong to--you still want the recognition
and respect as a human being."95

In the same speech, he also made clear
that the strategies were set apart by the
separatist advocacy of "by any means necessary."
Mrs. Betty Shabazz, the widow of Malcolm X,
explains the phrase this way:

> When Malcolm talked about black freedom,
> he meant freedom by whatever means. It
> is considered a point of honor for all peoples
> to defend their rights. . . . Malcolm
> believed in what Patrick Henry said: "I
> know not what course others may take; but

as for me, give me liberty or give me death!"96

Whereas King, the assimilationist, saw America as a "multiracial nation where all groups are dependent on each other" and in this interdependence no racial group could "retreat to an island entire of itself,"97 Malcolm believed the King approach was bound to fail because it appealed to instincts and qualities which were present in too few white Americans. The problem, as Malcolm saw it, was that in America blacks met few so-called "good" or "brotherly" white people. It was, therefore, the general "collective" body of whites that blacks had most to deal with.

Arguing the assimilationist approach was an "underdog . . . begging, hat-in-hand, compromising approach," Malcolm placed the struggle on a human rights level, observing that those blacks involved on the human rights level, "don't look upon themselves as Americans." In Malcolm's words:

> They look upon themselves as a part of dark mankind. They see the whole struggle not within the confines of the American stage, but . . . the whole stage. And, in the world context, they see that the dark man outnumbers the white man . . . the white man is just a microscopic minority.98

Therefore, argues Malcolm, the assimilationist "looks upon himself as a minority . . . because his scope is limited to the American scene," while the separatist sees himself "as part of the majority." And, says Malcolm, using a different approach to struggle for his rights,

> He doesn't beg . . . thank you for what you give him, because you are only giving him what he should have had a hundred years ago. He doesn't think you are doing him any favors. . . . Once . . . expanded . . .

to the level of human rights, it opens the
door for all of our brothers and sisters
in Africa and Asia, who have their independence, to come to our rescue.99

In review, separatist rhetoric identifies
itself with other nationalistic movements in
Asia, Africa, and Latin America in its call for
race unity, self-help, and self-determination.100

The separatist strategy is much like the
term nationalism in that it promotes the feeling
that racial groups ought to possess a country
of their own. Thus, groups sharing common
heritage, language, culture, as distinct from
other groups, should rule themselves and be in
control of their social, economic, and political
institutions. The rhetoric here implies that
blacks are a subjugated people and under the
control of a colonial government.101

The separatist also argues that full
integration or assimilation of blacks into the
white mainstream is "utopian" and never to be
realized. Therefore, the separatist argues:
Can separation be any less desirable than continued existence as second-class citizens?"102
Stressing the need for racial, cultural, and
psychological separation as a way of developing
a sense of racial integrity and black identity,
they preach, as Harland Randolph suggests, that
"each group must maintain its cultural
identity."103

Malcolm X was primarily responsible for
bringing the separatist message to great numbers
of blacks. He was also, until 1964, the chief
spokesman of the Black Muslims for the white
community. He states that America, for the
Black American, meant simply "prison." And for
the black auditor, he spoke the real truth for
many about the black status in America.104

Revolution

With the emergence of King as a moral
force in the struggle for equality, many Americans
looked forward to the day when prejudice and
racism would be replaced by the actuality of
brotherhood. But King was killed in 1968. Yet
even before his assassination, Arthur Smith suggests the civil rights movement appeared to be
exhausting itself.105 This decline in the nonviolence approach was accompanied by voices who
insisted on human rights for all Americans at
any cost whatsoever.106 The assassination of
Malcolm X also produced a number of potential
successors to the throne of radical protest.
These new revolutionists refined the tools of
protest and utilized the techniques of agita-
tional rhetoric to a greater degree than had
King, Wilkins, or Young, in their effort "to
liberate the black masses" from white
oppression.107 Among the major figures were
Stokley Carmichael, H. Rap Brown, and later
Eldridge Cleaver. Through television, news-
papers, and books, Carmichael argued that blacks
were oppressed as a group because they were
black. And he continued:

> . . . oppressed because we are black, .
> . . to get out . . . one must feel the group
> power that one has. Not the individual
> power which . . . is called in this country
> . . . integration.108

Addressing himself "to the problem of the many,"
he told a Berkeley audience in 1966:

> We cannot afford to be concerned about six
> percent of the children in this country
> . . . who you allow to come into white
> schools. We have 94 percent who still live
> in shacks. We are concerned about 94 per-
> cent. . . .
> . . . The question is, how can white
> society begin to move to see black people

32

as human beings? I am black, therefore
I am. Not that I am black and I must go
to college to prove myself. I am black,
therefore I am.[109]

With negotiation and compromise largely
discarded, Eldridge Cleaver interprets the situation in this more inclusive view:

Problems . . . can no longer be compromised
or swept cleverly under that national rug
of self-delusion. . . . Those who are
victimized by these "social problems"--
Negroes, the aged . . . poor . . . dis-
satisfied students, the haters of war and
lovers of man--have flung back the rug in
outranged rebellion, refusing to be silenced
until their grievances are uncompromisingly
redressed. America has come alive . . .
and . . . forces of revolutionary momentum
are squaring off in this land for decisive
showdowns from which no one can purchase
sanctuary.[110]

Willing to ally himself with all black, red,
white, and yellow people who think and act in
the revolutionary spirit as he does, Cleaver
believes the fundamental political problem facing
the world today is whether America moves decisively to the right or to the left. For Cleaver,
the true patriots may well be those individuals
on the "new left."[111]

As suggested previously, the term
"revolutionary rhetoric" is clearly one which
encourages a variety of interpretations.
Robert L. Scott has called this rhetoric "substantially justificatory" because it is "a
response to prior white violence"; it is "self-
defense" as it is a "reaction to racism around
the world" and "most readily identified with
guerilla action to overthrow imperialistic
colonialism." Further, it is "congruent with
the corrupt status quo in America."[112] Scott
concludes:

I believe that we must assume that their
rhetoric makes clear the world as it is
for many, perhaps most, Black Americans.
The ghetto is a colony; the White is the
enemy; a racist society is violent.113

A second interpretation of the term by
Gregg, McCormack, and Pedersen, contends that
revolutionary rhetoric "reflects the contemporary
situation as the black man perceives it, and
the black man's actions, like the behaviors of
us all, are decisively influenced by his percep-
tions." The rhetoric, then, is both an outgrowth
of and an agent-reaction on the society and
culture. These authors interpret the rhetoric
of the current black movement as a "kind of
parareligious catechism, to be believed because
it is so." The attacking and condemnation of
white society is "redundant" and appeals to
blackness are "often delivered as a litany."114
Viewed as "parareligious catechism," it also
offers the black man "a cathartic device for
the discovery of self."115

On the other hand, Arthur L. Smith believes
it is the "classic chasm" of "inconsistency
between ideal and reality, between theory and
practice" that gives this "aggressive rhetoric
its energy."116 Addison Gayle, Jr., author of
The Black Situation, explains the resolution
of this perceived inconsistency or conflict in
the mind of the revolutionary this way:

The moment arrives when this inner dichotomy
is resolved, when the forces of "desperate
rebellion" takes possession of his soul.
When this occurs he breaks his pact with
history, steps outside of it, becomes a
proponent of the impossible, an outlay;
which is to say, he becomes a revolu-
tionary.117

So, too, Thomas F. Pettigrew wrote in 1963:
"Intense relative deprivation in an age of rising

expectations is the stuff out of which revolutions are made."118

Charles U. Larson believes the rhetoric is clearly directed towards various audiences at different times. Larson explains that sometimes the message seems specifically designed for blacks; at other times directed to the white power structure, and, in yet other cases, aimed at blacks but meant to be overheard by whites.119

Put another way, Herbert W. Simons sees this strategy of persuasion as including the threat or employment of force.120 In the argument over reform versus revolution, the revolutionary realizes "that there's nothing like the threat of revolution to bring about some reforms."121

Black revolutionary rhetoric, explains Arthur Smith, has these features in common with any other rhetoric. First, this rhetoric is concerned with:

> . . . the communication of ideas, values, opinions, and beliefs in an effort to elicit the approval or acceptance of others. Within his particular situation, the rhetor attempts to discover means with which to show the aptness of his message. Insofar as the revolutionist seeks to find the means of pesuasion within a given rhetorical situation, he functions as a rhetor.122

Second, like all revolutionary rhetoric it

> . . . must possess an offensive stance if it is to mold the beliefs of the masses into a tight compact against the status quo opinion. Thus, all revolutionary rhetoric is essentially aggressive rather than defensive. The aggression inherent in revolutionary rhetoric becomes a unifying force that gives revolutionists a mien of tremendous energy.123

Third, "without grievance, distress, and political or social discomfort," a revolution, even a black revolution, "lacks the necessary fuel on which to base its power."[124]

It may be unique, however, in that first of all, it "speaks to and for the black masses," and, secondly, depends on the "linguistic components of the black language" as much as the grievances of the revolutionist. Third the revolutionary issues "a specialized call for community" with such phrases as "black is beautiful" and "let's get ourselves together" as important rallying expressions for unity. Fourth, concerned with identity, this rhetoric becomes "a rhetoric of redefinition" as they struggle with such terms as Afro-American, black, and brother. Essentially, argues Smith, the black revolutionists' aim is to preach pride, self-respect, and self-assertion, not only among themselves but with their "brothers" around the world. Fifth, believing that enslavement of the mind and spirit leaves the black masses helpless, the black communicator uses a militant rhetoric to change the black man's self-concept and humiliating image he has of himself. Sixth, where King's rhetoric was a "request," the revolutionists' is an "or else" demand, the only alternative being violence. Next, this rhetoric "possesses a militaristic outlook," or the style indicates, at least, a "reliance on military terminology."[125] Smith explains:

The rhetors have appropriated the language of revolution . . . to attain their rhetorical purpose. . . . Sloganizing is nothing less than a form of rhetorical aggression. To state a complex or intricate concept in a few simple emotional words is effectively to agitate: WE WANT BLACK POWER; MOVE ON OVER . . . ; HELL NO, WE WON'T GO.[126]

Last, this rhetoric has more emphasis on secular themes than earlier religious themes with the

acquisition of power superceding brotherhood
with the white community.127

On assimilation, the revolutionists argue
that there is no freedom in this strategy. They
seem antagonistic to persuasion as a method of
instituting social change and view integration
as a "deceitful plan" and totally unacceptable.128
Arguing from the premise that blacks form "an
oppressed colony in the midst of white America,"129
Cleaver sees himself as different from King and
other assimilationists in that those leaders
have been

> . . . willing to work within the . . . rules
> laid down by the white establishment. They
> have tried to bring change within the
> system . . . without violence. . . . Further-
> more, all are careful to remind everybody
> that they're Americans as well as "Negroes,"
> that the prestige of this country is as
> important to them as whites.130

Unlike King, he sees himself caring little about
preserving the dignity of a country that has
no regard for black dignity.131 Steps in
destroying the commitment to white society and
white cultural values involve:

1. No hair straightening.

2. The adoption of Afro hair styles and
clothes.

3. The attack on white grammatical verbal
values.132

On separatism, the revolutionists asserts
the good life cannot be attained by withdrawing
entirely into all black communities. In other
words, reaching the goals of the good life by
either leaving or joining society is impossible.
Revolution is the only way to improve the black
man's status. The removal of power from those
who have created the racist society through

37

violence, civil disobedience, and coercion then become both legitimate and necessary.[133]

Although not unique to black rhetoric, the message of destroying or tearing down the present society and replacing it with another is a basic ingredient in the black revolutionary message. As Eric Hoffer explains this tendency:

> The radical and the reactionary loathe the present. They see it as an aberration and a deformity. Both are ready to proceed ruthlessly and recklessly with the present, and both are hospitable to . . . self-scarifice. . . .
> The radical has a passionate faith in the infinite perfectibility of human nature. He believes that by changing man's environment . . . a society can be wrought that is wholly new and unprecedented.[134]

Another feature is to never make entirely clear one's plans for the future or telling the white enemy what one group is planning. As Hoffer again sees this strategy, its effectiveness as a doctrine does not come from its "meaning but from its certitude; that is, to be effective a doctrine must not be understood, but rather believed in. If neither unintelligible nor vague, it has to be unverifiable. When, says Hoffer, a movement begins to rationalize its doctrine and make it intelligible, it is a sign that its dynamic span is over and that it is now primarily interested in stability.[135]

The Inherent Evils of Whites

Golden and Rieke feel the following reoccurring themes are present in the black rhetoric of revolution:

1. The inherent evil of whites.

2. The inherent evils of capitalism.[136]

Citing hatred as the "most accessible and comprehensive of all unifying agents," Eric Hoffer provides this background material on the first theme. Mass movements, he writes, can never "rise and spread "without the "belief in a devil" as the strength of a movement is proportionate to the "vividness and tangibility of its devil." If, he continues, the enemy is vague, it is often necessary "to invent him." The ideal devil is also one who belongs to a single category enabling all hatred to be concentrated on a single foe. This ideal devil should also be "omnipotent and omnipresent" so that every difficulty and failure within the movement can be attributed to "the work of the devil."137

In the revolutionists' selection of white colonial America as the chosen enemy allies are also chosen. As Hoffer puts it:

> We do not usually look for allies when we love. . . . But we always look for allies when we hate. It is understandable that we should look for others to side with us when we have a just grievance and crave to retaliate against those who wronged us. . . . It is chiefly the reasonable hatreds that drive us to merge with those who hate as we do, and it is this kind of hatred that serves as one of the most effective cementing agents.138

Thus, in Hoffer's words, "hatred is a convenient instrument for mobilizing a community for defense" and a means of unification.139

Nothing that all true believers speak repeatedly on the decadence of Western democracies, Hoffer concludes:

> There are a deep reassurance for the frustrated in witnessing the down-fall of the fortunate and the disgrace of the righteous. They see in a general down-fall an approach to the brotherhood of

all. . . . Their burning conviction that
there must be a new life and a new order
is fueled by the realization that the
old will have to be razed to the ground
before the new can be built. Their clamor
for a millennium is shot through with
hatred for all that exists, and a craving
for the end of the world.140

Cleaver reflects the implications of Hoffer's
above remark with the words: "We shall have
our manhood. We shall have it or the earth will
be leveled by our attempts to gain it."141

The Inherent Evils of Capitalism

An examination of the second theme, the
inherent evils of capitalism, reveals that the
black rhetoric of revolution is much like the
anti-colonialism message preached by many communist leaders. It seems akin to communist
ideology in that both stress the interdependence
and interresponsibility of man, both profess
that real participation should be at the grass-
roots or worker level, both are international
and revolutionary movements, and for both, the
ultimate goal is worldly. Although one cannot
say these ingredients or similar messages make
the black radical a communist, these further
parallels can be drawn:

1. Both blame capitalism for world
problems and the conditions of man.

2. Both say capitalism is exploitative.

3. Both preach an anti-colonialism message.

4. Both advocate violent revolution to
overthrow the existing system.

The following lines from Cleaver's interview with Lee Lockwood are suggestive of this
attitude:

I'm saying an American application of the
principles of socialism that hopes to move
to the classless society . . . that we have
to do away with the institution of private
property . . . have an equal distribution
of the products of our industry and our
technology. . . . I'm saying that what we
need to do is to rearrange the system .
. . need . . . a war on the rich . . . on
the system of the rich . . . on the system
that allows proverty to exist in the midst
of all those riches.142

It is within the context of this second
theme one can write that today's black rhetoric
of revolution is not altogether an original or
unique rhetoric. Appearing a socialistic movement tied to the general worldwide class struggles
taking place, it is not unique in that the arguments advanced are essentially drawn from a col-
lection of ideas by such revolutionaries as Mao,
Fanon, Lenin, Che Guevara, with Malcolm X supply-
ing the black arguments. These ideas seek to
establish the colonialist character of black
Americans, oppressed in ways similar to the
laboring and peasant classes everywhere under
the control of corporations, land monopolies,
and capitalistic materialism. Attacking the
capitalist system which allows landlords and
owners to grow rich through the labor of the
black poor, spokesmen for the Black Panther party
who envision the establishment of a socialist
state, argue the revolution is indeed a class
war and must include all oppressed peoples.
Carmichael argues blacks are engaged in a color
war. Importantly, however, these ideas, while
not original altogether with the black American,
are then seen by some black advocates as
analagous and applicable to the black problem
in America. Yet, as Roy Wilkins sees this group
of advocates: "They're a little behind the
times. Some of their socialism sounds like the
1930s and sounds like they've just discovered
it."143

What must be particularly noted is the
black revolutionist's high regard for the writings
of Frantz Fanon, the African-born, French-
educated psychiatrist who became a revolutionary
theorist during the Algerian rebellion. Fanon's
The Wretched of the Earth, regarded by Cleaver,
Carmichael, and others as "a classic study of
the psychology of oppressed peoples," has now
become known among the militants of the black
liberation movement in America as the primary
handbook for the black revolution and, as Cleaver
admits, "The Black Bible."[144] The main thrust
by Fanon is his emphasis on the idea that
colonialism and its resulting subjugation,
physical exploitation, and psychological devalua-
tion, cannot be overcome by peaceful means
because the oppressed must undergo a sense of
transformation in terms of self-image. Fanon
urges that violence can be, by itself, "a
cleansing force" in this transformation. He
sees violence as freeing "the native from his
inferiority complex and from his despair and
inaction; it makes him fearless, and restores
his self-respect."[145] In another way, violence
lets man recreate himself. Comparable to a
"royal pardon," the colonized man finds his
freedom in and through violence.[146]

Cleaver frequently alludes to Fanon's
point that blacks can wrest their manhood from
white society only through revolutionary
political struggle, not through posturing, dress,
or reviving African cultural roots.[147] He sees
Fanon providing a great service to revolutionaries
by explaining and analyzing how colonized peoples
move from an awareness of being oppressed to
the ultimate height of consciousness where they
are willing to fight for their freedom. Also
important to Cleaver is how Fanon legitimizes
and destroys feelings of guilt one might have
over wanting to kill his master. Thus, in
destroying the idea that there is something wrong
with the revolutionary impulse, Cleaver sees
the book as valuable in its endorsement of

violence to remove "the oppressor's boot off your neck."148

As Cleaver sees Fanon's stages of libera-tion, he writes that oppressed people feel an uncontrollable desire to kill their masters. But in shrinking from this impulse, the violence is often turned upon itself and the oppressed people fight among themselves. At this stage, the internalized violence of oppressed people produces the major distortions in the personality.149

Cleaver notes that what Fanon importantly teaches is to focus all the hatred and violence on the true target--the oppressor. As murder, Cleaver writes, can strangely make the oppressed sane again, he feels the Fanon book importantly legitimizes the revolutionary impulse to violence and further

> teaches colonial subjects that it is per-fectly normal for them to want to rise up and cut off the heads of the slave masters, that it is a way to achieve their manhood, and that they must oppose the oppressor in order to experience themselves as men.150

Cleaver's major thesis is that American society is one of the gun and that it evolves around muscle and brute force. Yet it is incumbent upon Cleaver, observes Gayle, to also believe that men are more victims of systems than the originators of them and that no man is inherently evil.151 Thus, Cleaver also speaks of the need for radical whites to develop some-thing to which blacks can relate to so that a meaningful coalition can be formed.152 On the coalition question itself, Mike Wallace, CBS news correspondent, reported on the program "60 Minutes" broadcast, January 6, 1970, that

> Whatever else the Panthers may teach, they do not teach racism. They do not teach black supremacy, . . . black separatism.

43

They talk about the problems of the poor,
all the poor, not just blacks.[153]

Importantly, Cleaver views the development
of the Black Panther party as stemming directly
from what Malcolm X taught.[154]

Malcolm X advocated that black people arm
themselves in a political fashion in order
to protect themselves when they move for
their rights. Malcolm made the shift of
emphasis from civil rights to human rights,
and he put the great emphasis on the need
for black people to arm themselves so that
they could defend themselves against the
attacks that were being made at that time.[155]

On this point, Cleaver, Huey Newton, and Bobby
Seale, see themselves as "trying to salvage the
effort that was being made by Malcolm and to
perpetuate it."[156]

Cleaver's basic demand is for proportionate
participation in the real power that runs America.
This means for Cleaver black people must have
part of the decision-making power concerning
all legislation, all appropriations of money,
and foreign policy.[157] Admitting he and the
Panthers are revolutionary, this also means,
he states:

We're disciplined, that we're working out
programs, that we intend to create a radical
political machinery in coalition with whites
that will uproot this decadent society,
transform its politics and economics and
build a structure fit to exist on a civilized
planet inhabited by humanized beings.[158]

Cleaver's speeches generally center on
his assumption that black people in America form
an oppressed colony. To white society, he makes
clear that "it is the conduct of whites, not
their skin color, that he condemns."[159] In this

44

context, then, "the oppressor has no rights which the oppressed are bound to respect." The essential question for white Americans then becomes: "Which side do you choose? Do you side with the oppressor or with the oppressed? The time for decision is upon you." Thus, as Cleaver perceives the situation, a choice is present in his rhetoric. Whites are either with the black American's drive for freedom or against him. In this framework, he can then warn: "But there is a choice and it will be made, by decision or indecision, by action or inaction, by commission or omission."[160]

While King believed the nonviolent approach would most effectively bring blacks into the mainstream of American life as quickly as possible, Cleaver, on the other hand, advocates the total, unequivocal destruction of capitalism and in its place a socialist system that would be compatible with the "spirit" of the American people and conditions that exist in America.[161] Drawn from Cleaver's interview with Lee Lockwood, author of Castro's Cuba, Cuba's Fidel, and the first American photographer inside North Vietnam after the war began, he explains further that he wants an American application of the principles of socialism that hopes to move to the classless society; that is, a "Yankee-Doodle-Dandy version" that will fit America's particular situation.[162] Cleaver realizes the examples of other revolutions cannot be entirely applied to the situation in America. Believing "our situation is unique," classical revolutionary principles and models, he feels, can be followed only when analogous to the black problem. He, thus, elaborates a theory of revolution that will cope with the highly urbanized, highly mechanized, industrialized society that blacks live in and says: "I am very critical of what I call 'revolutionary romanticism' . . . walking around the cities in combat boots and fatigue jackets . . . unfortunately this is not functional in an urban situation."[163] Cleaver believes it more functional for revolutionaries in the urban

setting to study the model of the Mafia to see
how they move in the cities and "function in
terms of arms in an organized fashion." Conse-
quently, the black urban guerilla has a respon-
sibility to look at the terrain, urban geography,
because the only models of revolutionary behavior
blacks have are those taken from rural terrain.164

The goal, he remarks, "is to bring heaven
down to earth." He, too, seeks "the good life"
by creating "the best possible living conditions
and standards of living that human knowledge
and technology are capable of providing." He
maintains this is both the aspiration and the
dream of the revolutionary. Assuring his
audiences that socialism would not turn America
into a satellite of the Soviet Union or Americans
into Chinese or Cuban people, it would instead
only put the American people on a basis where
they can be friends with the people of Russia,
China, Cuba, in fact, with the people of the
whole world.165

Cleaver still "admires the American Con-
stitution and believes in the American Dream."
Yet, he is convinced that socialism can succeed
in America where it has failed abroad because
Americans possess "such a strong tradition of
democracy" they would never permit "a system
that infringed on their civil liberties."166

In establishing his "Yankee-Doodle-Dandy"
form of socialism for the future, Cleaver foresees
the revolution spearheaded by bloody urban
guerilla warfare. Insisting this has already
begun and "intensifying steadily," he holds that
as the "forces of reaction escalate their
repression," there will be a right-wing coup
d'etat in this country. This act, he contends,
will trigger the final, all-out conflict which
will bring the revolution to power.167

One final quality that Cleaver exhibits
in common with other revolutionaries is the
willingness to die for his cause. The following

remark from Stokely Carmichael is suggestive
of this attitude:

> Brother Malcolm used to tell us that there
> were seveal types of death. I think a
> dehumanized people who do not fight back
> are a dead people. That is what the West
> has been able to do to most of us. They
> dehumanized us to the point where we would
> not even fight back. Once you have begun
> to fight back, you are alive, . . . and
> bullets do not kill you. If you do not
> fight back, you are dead. . . . So we are
> alive today, . . . all over the world. All
> of our black people are coming alive because
> they are fighting back. They are fighting
> for their humanity. . . . When you become
> alive, you want to live so much that you
> fight to live. See, when you are dead .
> . . do not rebel, you are not fighting to
> live, you are already dead. Well, we are
> alive and we love life so much that we are
> willing to die for it. So, we are alive.
> Death cannot stop us.[168]

Believing that "a revolutionary is a doomed man,"
Cleaver, too, affirms that if one is not "willing
to put your life on the line" and come to terms
with the prospects of death, then, as a revolutionary, "you have no business at all in defying
or confronting or even arguing with the power
structure." Thus, the revolutionary comes to
terms with the idea he may be killed at any
time.[169]

In review, the revolutionist argues that
there is no freedom for blacks in either
absorption into white society or withdrawing
into all black communities.[170] The message for
blacks is that violence, coercion, and civil
disobedience are "legitimate and necessary."
For the white audience, the black speaker
emphasizes the choice between violence or
peaceful settlement is up to white America.
Employing what Golden and Rieke term "a rhetoric

of preparation," the black orator makes clear that choice is in the hands of white Americans.[171]

The rhetorical goals of the revolutionist are to develop a sense of brotherhood among blacks, to emphasize that people of "color" constitute a world majority, and to make the prospect of ultimate victory seem real.

The reoccurring themes are:

1. The inherent evils of whites and capitalism.

2. Black Americans are a colonized people.

3. Integration is unacceptable for achieving the good life.

4. Revolution is necessary.

5. Violence is justified.[172]

NOTES: THE RHETORICAL STRATEGIES
OF BLACK AMERICANS

[1]John Hope Franklin and Roger Butterfield, "The Search for a Black Past," Life, 22 November 1968, p. 91.

[2]Ibid.

[3]Vito Silvestri, "Emma Goldman, Enduring Voice of Anarchism," Today's Speech 17 (September 1969):20.

[4]Smith, "Building a Course in Black History: A Rhetorical Perspective," p. 19.

[5]Smith, Rhetoric of Black Revolution (Boston: Allyn & Bacon, 1969), p. 105.

[6]Joanne Grant, ed., Black Protest, Fawcett Premier Books (New York: Fawcett Publications, 1968), p. 8.

[8]Hortense Powdermaker, "The Channeling of Negro Aggression by the Cultural Process," in vol. 2 of The Making of Black America, ed. August Meier and Elliott Rudwick (New York: Atheneum Press, 1969), p. 94.

[8]Ibid., pp. 94-95.

[9]King, Where Do We Go From Here: Chaos or Community? p. 163.

[10]Ibid.

[11]Robert L. Scott and Wayne Brockriede, The Rhetoric of Black Power (New York: Harper & Row, 1969), p. 1.

[12]Ibid., pp. 2-3.

[13] Ibid., pp. 202-4.

[14] Richard L. Johannesen, review of Rhetoric of Black Revolution, by Arthur L. Smith, in Today Speech 18 (Winter 1970):49.

[15] Smith, Black Revolution, p. 26.

[16] Ibid., pp. 26-40.

[17] Ibid., p. 50.

[18] Harland L. Randolph, "Inter-group Communication: How Negroes Estimate the Attitudes of Whites Toward Them," Today's Speech 8 (November 1960):30.

[19] Ibid., p. 31.

[20] "The Terms Defined," Ebony, August 1970, p. 35.

[21] Ibid.

[22] Ibid.

[23] Ibid.

[24] Smith, "Building a Course in Black History: A Rhetorical Perspective," pp. 19-20.

[25] Robert N. Manning, "The Use of War and Peace in the Basic College Speech Course," Today's Speech 17 (September 1969):39.

[26] Roger Butterfield, "A Separate Path to Equality," Life, 13 December 1968, p. 82.

[27] Jamye Coleman Williams, "A Rhetorical Anslysis of Thurgood Marshall's Arguments Before the Supreme Court in the Public School Segregation Controversy" (Ph.D. dissertation, The Ohio State University, 1959), pp. 72, 76-78. A transcript of the oral arguments of Marshall before the Supreme Court on December 7 and 8, 1953,

covers pp. 276-316 in the dissertation. The
Opinion of the Supreme Court: <u>Brown v. Board of
Education</u>, May 17, 1954, covers pp. 267-75 in
the dissertation.

[28]Butterfield, "Separate Path," p. 82.
See also James H. Laue, "The Changing Character
of Negro Protest," in <u>Black Revolt: Strategies
of Protest</u>, ed. by Doris Y. Wilkinson (Berkeley:
McCutchan Publishing Corporation, 1969),
pp. 65-69.

[29]King, <u>Where Do We Go</u>.

[30]Mr. Storey is a graduate of Harvard
College, a trustee of Exeter Academy, and a
trustee of the Ohio Foundation of Independent
Colleges.

[31]Robert Storey, "Goodbye, Booker T.,"
<u>Beacon Magazine</u> of Emerson College, Spring 1970,
p. 17.

[32]Ibid.

[33]Ibid., pp. 17-18.

[34]Ibid., p. 18.

[35]Smith, <u>Black Revolution</u>, p. 17.

[36]King, "Nonviolence and Racial Justice,"
<u>Christian Century</u> 74 (February 6, 1957):165-67.

[37]Ibid.

[38]Smith, <u>Black Revolution</u>, pp. 19-29.

[39]King <u>Where Do We Go</u>, p. 73.

[40]Ibid., pp. 74-77.

[41]Ibid., pp. 144-45.

[42]Ibid., p. 50.

[43] Ibid.

[44] Ibid., p. 153.

[45] Powdermaker, "Channeling of Negro Aggression," p. 99.

[46] Ibid., pp. 100-1.

[47] Eric Hoffer, The True Believer, Perennial Library (New York: Harper & Row, 1951), p. 19.

[48] Ibid., p. 68.

[49] Lewis M. Killian and Charles U. Smith, "Negro Protest Leaders in a Southern Community," in vol. 2 of The Making of Black America, ed. Meier and Rudwick (New York: Atheneum Press, 1969), p. 334-35.

[50] Jack Walker, "The Functions of Disunity: Negro Leadership in a Soutnern City," in vol. 2 of The Making of Black America, ed. Meier and Rudwick (New York: Atheneum Press, 1969), pp. 348, 342.

[51] August Meier, "On the Role of Martin Luther King," in vol. 2 of The Making of Black America, ed. Meier and Rudwick (New York: Atheneum Press, 1969), p. 353.

[52] Ibid., pp. 354-55.

[53] Ibid.

[54] Ibid., pp. 355-61.

[55] Scott and Brockriede, Black Power, p. 198.

[56] Herbert W. Simons, "Patterns of Persuasion in the Civil Right Struggle," Today's Speech 15 (February 1967):26.

[57] Golden and Rieke, Rhetoric of Black Americans, pp. 141, 270, 43.

[58] Ibid., pp. 43-52, 170-71.

[59] Ibid., pp. 270-71.

[60] Charles E. Fager, "Dilemma for Dr. King," Christian Century 88 (March 16, 1966): 331.

[61] Ibid.

[62] Lawrence P. Neal, "Black Power in the International Context," in The Black Power Revolt, ed. Floyd B. Barbour (Toronto: Collier-MacMillan Co., 1968), p. 159.

[63] Hans J. Massaquoi, "Elijah Muhammad: Prophet and Architect of the Separate Nation of Islam," Ebony, August 1970, p. 78.

[64] Butterfield, "Separate Path," p. 82.

[65] Ibid.

[66] C. Eric Lincoln, The Black Muslims in America, rev. ed. (Boston: Beacon Press, 1973), p. 246.

[67] Ibid., p. 4.

[68] Ibid., pp. 22-23. See also Elijah Muhammad, "Are We The Black Muslims?" Muhammad Speaks, 25 April 1969, p. 19.

[69] Ibid., pp. 22-27.

[70] Ibid., pp. 27-30.

[71] Muhammad, "The Muslim Program," Muhammad Speaks, 25 April 1969, p. 40.

[72] Lincoln, Black Muslims, pp. 33-34.

[73] Ibid., pp. 44-46.

[74] Muhammad, "Negro," Muhammad Speaks, 25 April 1969, p. 21.

[75] Muhammad, "Separation Is A Must," Muhammad Speaks, 25 April 1969, p. 20.

[76] Lincoln, Black Muslims, pp. 67-72, 220.

[77] Muhammad, "The Muslim Program," p. 40; see also Lincoln, Black Muslims, pp. 84-97.

[78] Lincoln, Black Muslims, pp. 121-22.

[79] Ibid., p. 115. The selectivity of Muslim names is developed at length in the regularly published article Muhammad, "Why Black Man Should Be Called By the Names of God," Muhammad Speaks, 25 April 1969, p. 21.

[80] Ibid., p. 129.

[81] Ibid., pp. 151-53, 186-87.

[82] Ibid., pp. 199, 217-18. A similar point of view is developed at length by Gerturde Samuels, "Two Ways: Black Muslim and N.A.A.C.P.," in Black Protest in the Sixties, ed. Meier and Rudwick (Chicago: Quadrangle Books, 1970), pp. 37-45.

[83] Storey, "Goodbye, Booker, T.," p. 18.

[84] Ibid.

[85] Lincoln, The Black Muslims, pp. 189-95.

[86] Malcolm X (with the assistance of Alex Haley), The Autobiography of Malcolm X (New York: Grover Press, 1966), p. 266.

[87] Ibid., p. 374.

[88] Butterfield, "Separate Path," p. 82.

[89]Fletcher Knebel, "A Visit with the Widow of Malcolm X," Look, 4 March 1969, p. 77. For a thorough description of Malcolm's scholarly activities in prison, see his autobiography, pp. 151-90.

[90]Knebel, "Widow of Malcolm X," p. 77. For a more detailed account of those influences that altered his later view of white society, see his autobiography, pp. 288-377, 413.

[91]George Brietman, ed., Malcolm X Speaks (New York: Grover Press, 1965), p. 51.

[92]Malcolm X, Autobiography, p. 272.

[93]Breitman, Malcolm X Speaks, p. 51.

[94]Ibid.

[95]Ibid., p. 116.

[96]Knebel, "Widow of Malcolm X," p. 74.

[97]King, Where Do We Go, p. 71.

[98]Brietman, Malcolm X Speaks, p. 52.

[99]Ibid., pp. 52-53.

[100]Golden and Rieke, Black Americans, pp. 43-44, 279-80.

[101]Ibid., pp. 280-81.

[102]Ibid., pp. 282-83.

[103]Randolph, "Inter-Group Communication," p. 30.

[104]Golden and Rieke, Black Americans, pp. 411-421-22.

[105]Smith, Black Revolution, pp. vi, 17.

[106] Ibid., p. vi.

[107] Ibid., p. 19.

[108] Cited in Storey, "Goodbye, Booker T.," p. 18.

[109] Ibid., pp. 18-19.

[110] Eldridge Cleaver, Soul on Ice, Delta Books (New York: Dell Publishing Co., 1968), pp. 112-13.

[111] Ibid., p. 114.

[112] Scott and Brockriede, Black Power, p. 134.

[113] Ibid., p. 143.

[114] Richard B. Gregg, A. Jackson McCormack, and Douglas J. Pedersen, "The Rhetoric of Black Power: A Street-Level Interpretation," Quarterly Journal of Speech 55 (April 1969): 151-58.

[115] Charles U. Larson, "The Trust Establishing Function of the Rhetoric of Black Power," Central States Speech Journal 21 (Spring 1970):52.

[116] Smith, "Henry Highland Garnet: Black Revolutionary in Sheep's Vestments," Central States Speech Journal 21 (Summer 1970):96.

[117] Addison Gayle, Jr., The Black Situation (New York: Horizon Press, 1970), p. 210.

[118] Thomas F. Pettigrew, "Actual Gains and Psychological Losses: The Negro American Protest," in vol. 2 of The Making of Black America, ed. Meier and Rudwick (New York: Atheneum Press, 1969), p. 325.

[119] Larson, "Trust Establishing Function," p. 52.

[120]Simons, "Patterns of Persuasion,"
p. 26.

[121]Per Fageron, "A Dip Into the Sea,"
Beacon Magazine of Emerson College, Spring 1970,
p. 31. See also Ralph J. Bunche, "The Programs
of Organizations Deveoted to the Improvement of
the Status of the American Negro," in vol. 2 of
The Making of Black America, ed. Meier and
Rudwick (New York: Antheneum Press, 1969),
p. 256.

[122]Smith, Black Revolution, pp. 1-2.

[123]Ibid., p. 1.

[124]Ibid.

[125]Ibid., pp. 1-21.

[126]Ibid., p. 21.

[127]Ibid., pp. 48-49, 87.

[128]Golden and Rieke, Black Americans,
pp. 44, 453, 515.

[129]Robert Scheer, ed., Eldridge Cleaver:
Post Prison Writings and Speeches (New York:
Random House, 1969), pp. xi, 61.

[130]Nat Hentoff, "Playboy Interview:
Eldridge Cleaver," Playboy, December 1968, p. 90.

[131]Ibid.

[132]Golden and Rieke, Black Americans,
p. 497.

[133]Ibid., pp. 44-45, 517.

[134]Hoffer, The True Believer, p. 71.

[135]Ibid., pp. 76-77.

[136] Golden and Rieke, Black Americans, pp. 503-5.

[137] Hoffer, The True Believer, pp. 85-87.

[138] Ibid., p. 88.

[139] Ibid., pp. 91-93.

[140] Ibid., pp. 91-92, 147.

[141] Cleaver, Soul on Ice, p. 61.

[142] Lee Lockwood, Conversation with Eldridge Cleaver--Algiers, Delta Books (New York: Dell Publishing Co., 1970), pp. 63z64.

[143] "60 Minutes," CBS telecast, January 6, 1970: "The Black Panthers," Narrator Mike Wallace.

[144] Scheer, Post-Prison Writings, p. 18.

[145] Frantz Fanon, The Wretched of the Earth, trans. by Constance Farrington (New York: Grove Press, 1968), p. 94.

[146] Ibid., pp. 21, 86.

[147] Scheer, Post-Prison Writings, p. xi.

[148] Lockwood, Conversation, pp. 90-91.

[149] Scheer, Post-Prison Writings, pp. 18-19.

[150] Ibid., p. 20.

[151] Gayle, Jr., The Black Situation, p. 215.

[152] Smith, Black Revolution, pp. 108-9.

[153] "60 Minutes," January 6, 1970, p. 5.

[154] Lockwood, Conversation, p. 86.

[155] Ibid.

[156] Ibid.

[157] Hentoff, "Playboy Interview," p. 90.

[158] Ibid., p. 104.

[159] Scheer, Post-Prison Writings,
pp. xii-xiii.

[160] Ibid., pp. 38-39.

[161] Lockwood, Conversation, p. 65.

[162] Ibid., pp. 63-64.

[163] Ibid., pp. 51-52.

[164] Ibid., p. 52.

[165] Ibid., pp. 63-65.

[166] Ibid., pp. 27-28.

[167] Ibid., pp. 28-29.

[168] Cited in Golden and Rieke, Black
Americans, pp. 534-35.

[169] Lockwood, Conversation, pp. 37-38.

[170] Golden and Rieke, Black Americans,
p. 44.

[171] Ibid., pp. 455, 45.

[172] Ibid., pp. 497-522.

CONCLUSIONS

The black American established an Afro-American presence in the everyday life of America during the decades of the sixties and seventies. Blacks believed, more than ever, their words had the power and impact to change people and events. While they did not achieve much in the way of establishing decision-making power as such, some decisions on both the local and national levels were now being made with the black community in mind.

Second, black communication has been evolutionary rather than revolutionary. It has recently turned from a singular concern with conditions in America to a more global, universal concern with human rights throughout the world. Black speakers increasingly speak not of a national minority but an international majority, linking and aligning themselves with newly emerging Third World countries opposed to colonialism and oppression.

Third, while the black freedom movement reinvigorated and restored some morality to an increasingly purposeless, valueless, and alienated American society, fractionalization, suspicion, and division remains characteristic of black leadership today. No elected black official substantially influences decisions on the national level. Blacks remain unable or unwilling to organize themselves politically. Disunity and hopelessness describe the situation. Hundreds of thousands never vote. Therefore, a general conclusion about black rhetoric, regardless of the spokesperson, strategy, or the issue, is the continuing lack of cohesiveness and unity at all levels. No one organization or individual speaks for the black community or makes effective use of the numerical strength of the black

population. One is hard pressed to decide whether
Andrew Young, Jesse Jackson, or Benjamin Hooks,
is the major black leader in America in the early
eighties.

Finally, special attention should be given
to inner-city black youth. Faced with high
black teenage unemployment, cutbacks in social
programs, rising inflation, poor housing, sub-
standard schools, high black-on-black crime,
and the influx of Cuban, Haitian, Mexican, and
other illegal aliens, many now feel urban America
should be the black man's battleground. Possessing
a new awareness of self and his or her priorities
in life, these urban, young blacks more than
ever believe America owes them something. Thus,
short on patience, it may well be for the eighties
that the most seriously listened to blacks in
America will be the angry young blacks confined
to America's inner cities.

BIBLIOGRAPHY

Books

Breitman, George, ed. Malcolm X. Speaks. New
York: Grover Press, 1965.

Cleaver, Eldridge. Soul on Ice. Delta Books.
New York: Dell Publishing Co., 1968.

Fanon, Frantz. The Wretched of the Earth.
Translated by Costance Farrington.
New York: Grover Press, 1968.

Gayle, Jr., Addison. The Black Situation.
New York: Horizon Press, 1970.

Golden, James L., and Rieke, Richard D. The
Rhetoric of Black Americans. Columbus,
Ohio: Charles E. Merrill Co., 1971.

Grant, Joanne, ed. Black Protest: History,
Documents, and Analysis, 1619 to the
Present. Fawcett Premier Books. New York:
Fawcett Publications, 1968.

Hoffer, Eric. The True Believer. Perennial
Library. New York: Harper & Row, 1951.

King, Martin Luther. Where Do We Go From Here:
Chaos or Community? Bantam Books.
New York: Harper & Row, 1968.

Lincoln, C. Eric. The Black Muslims in America.
Boston: Beacon Press, 1961.

Lockwood, Lee. Conversation with Eldridge
Cleaver in Algiers. Delta Books. New
York: Dell Publishing Co., 1970.

Mullen, Robert W. Blacks and Vietnam. Lanham,
    Maryland: University Press of America,
    1981.

_____. Blacks in America's Wars.
    New York: Monad Press, 1973.

_____. Rhetorical Strategies of Black
    Americans. Lanham, Maryland: University
    Press of America, 1980.

Scheer, Robert, ed. Eldridge Cleaver: Post-
    Prison Writings and Speeches. New York:
    Random House, 1969.

Scott, Robert L., and Brockriede, Wayne. The
    Rhetoric of Black Power. New York:
    Harper & Row, 1969.

Smith, Arthur L. Rhetoric of Black Revolution.
    Boston: Allyn & Bacon, 1969.

X., Malcolm, and Haley, Alex. The Autobiography
    of Malcolm X. New York: Grove Press,
    1966.

Articles and Journals

"Black America 1970." Time, 6 April 1970,
    pp. 13-35, 45-100.

Butterfield, Roger. "The Mobilization of Black
    Strength." Life 6 December 1968,
    pp. 93-106.

_____. "A Separate Path to Equality." Life,
    13 December 1968, pp. 82-98.

Carmichael, Stokley. "Black Power and the Third
    World." Printed in a pamphlet by the
    Southern Student Organizing Committee,
    Nashville, Tennessee, 1967, pp. 1-10.

Carmichael, Stokley. "Power and Racism." Printed
in a pamphlet by the Southern Student
Organizating Committee, Nashville,
Tennessee, 1966, pp. 1-9.

Fager, Charles E. "Dilemma for Dr. King."
Christian Century 83 (March 16, 1966):
331-32.

Fageron, Per. "A Dip into the Sea." Beacon
Magazine of Emerson College, Spring 1970,
pp. 25-31.

Franklin, John Hope, and Butterfield, Roger.
"The Search for a Black Past." Life,
22 November 1968, pp. 90-120.

Gregg, Richard B.; McCormack, A. Jackson; and
Pedersen, Douglas J. "The Rhetoric of
Black Power: A Street Level Interpreta-
tion." Quarterly Journal of Speech 55
(April 1969):151-60.

Hentoff, Nat. "Playboy Interview: Eldridge
Cleaver." Playboy, December 1968, pp. 89-
108, 238.

Johannesen, Richard L. Review of Rhetoric of
Black Revolution, by Arthur L. Smith.
Today's Speech 18 (Winter 1970):49.

King, Martin Luther. "A Time to Break Silence."
Freedomways 7 (Spring 1967):103-17.

_____. "Speeches by the Reverend Doctor
Martin Luther King, Jr., about the War in
Vietnam." Annandale, Virginia: The
Turnpike Press, pp. 1-25.

_____. "Nonviolence and Racial Justice."
Christian Century 74 (February 6, 1957):
165-67.

Knebel, Fletcher. "A Visit with the Widow of
Malcolm X." Look, 4 March 1969, pp. 74-80.

Larson, Charles U. "The Trust Establishing
Function of the Rhetoric of Black Power."
Central States Speech Journal 21 (Spring
1970):52-56.

Lester, Julius. "The Angry Children of Malcolm X."
Printed in a pamphlet by the Southern
Student Organizing Committee, Nashville,
Tennessee, 1966, pp. 1-9.

Manning, Robert N. "The Use of War and Peace
in the Basic College Speech Course."
Today's Speech 17 (September 1969):37-42.

Massaquoi, Hans J. "Elijah Muhammad: Prophet
and Architect of the Separate Nation of
Islam." Ebony, August 1970, p. 78.

"Muhammad Ali--the Measure of a Man." Freedomways 7 (Spring 1967):101-2.

Muhammad Speaks, 25 April 1969.

Newton, Huey P. "The Black Panther Party."
Ebony, August 1969, pp. 107-12.

_____. "Huey Newton Talks to the Movement."
Interview originally published in Movement, August 1968. Printed in a pamphlet
by Students for a Democratic Society,
August 1968, pp. 4-14.

O'Dell, J. H. "The Contours of the 'Black
Revolution' in the 1970's." Freedomways
10 (Second Quarter, 1970):104-14.

Parks, Gordon. "Eldridge Cleaver in Algiers,
A Visit with Papa Rage." Life
6 February 1970, pp. 20-25.

Randolph, Harland L. "Inter-Group Communication:
How Negroes Establish the Attitudes of
Whites Towards Them." Today's Speech 8
(November 1960):28-31.

"Report From Black America--A Newsweek Poll."
     Newsweek, 30 June 1969, pp. 16-35.

Silvestri, Vito. "Emma Goldman, Enduring
     Voice of Anarchism." Today's Speech 17
     (September 1969):20-25.

Simons, Herbert W. "Patterns of Persuasion in
     the Civil Rights Struggle." Today's
     Speech 15 (February 1967):25-27.

"60 Minutes," CBS Telecast, January 6, 1970:
     "The Black Panthers." Narrator Mike
     Wallace.

Smith, Arthur L. "Building a Course in Black
     History: A Rhetorical Perspective."
     Abstract of paper presented at the 55th
     meeting of the Speech Association of
     America, New York City, December 27,
     1969, pp. 19-20.

_____. "Henry Highland Garnet: Black
     Revolutionary in Sheep's Vestments."
     Central States Speech Journal 21
     (Summer 1970):93-98.

Storey, Robert. "Goodbye, Booker T." Beacon
     Magazine of Emerson College, Spring 1970,
     pp. 17-20.

"The Terms Defined." Ebony, August 1970, p. 35.

INDEX

ABOUT THE AUTHOR

Robert W. Mullen is Associate Professor of Speech Communication at Northern Kentucky University, Highland Heights, Kentucky. He received his B.S. and M.S. degrees in Speech from Emerson College in Boston and his Ph.D. from The Ohio State University in 1971. His dissertation in rhetoric and public address was titled <u>Issues Developed by Select Black Americans on the Vietnam War</u>.

Dr. Mullen is also the author of <u>Blacks in America's Wars</u>, Monad Press, New York, 1973, <u>The Rhetorical Strategies of Black Americans</u>, University Press of America, Maryland, 1980, and <u>Blacks and Vietnam</u>, Univerity Press of America, Maryland, 1981.

He is married to Dianna Delgado of Chicago and American Airlines, and presently lives in Newport, Kentucky.